DATE DUE		

The Ant and the Grasshopper

RETOLD AND ILLUSTRATED BY

Amy Lowry Poole

HOLIDAY HOUSE / New York

This book was designed by Claire Counihan and set in Hiroshige.
The artwork was painted with ink and gouache on rice paper.

Library of Congress Cataloging-in-Publication Data
Poole, Amy Lowry.
The ant and the grasshopper / retold and illustrated by Amy Lowry Poole.—1st ed.
p.   cm.
Summary: Retells the fable about a colony of industrious ants which
busily prepares for the approaching winter while a grasshopper makes
no plans for the cold weather to come.
ISBN 0-8234-1477-9
[1. Fables. 2. Folklore.] I. Aesop. II. Title.
Pz8.2.P545An 2000
398.24'525726—dc21
[E]   99-18820
CIP

In memory of my father,
Donald Irwin Lowry (1920–1999)

A LONG TIME AGO, in the old Summer Palace at the edge of the Emperor's courtyard, there lived a grasshopper and a family of ants.

The ants awoke every day before dawn and began their endless tasks of rebuilding their house of sand, which had been washed down by the evening rains, and searching for food, which they would store beneath the ground.

They carried their loads grain by grain,
one by one, back and forth, all day long.

The grasshopper liked to sleep
late into the morning, rising as the sun
stretched toward noon.

"Silly ants," he would say. "You work too hard. Come follow me into the courtyard, where I will sing and dance for the great Emperor."

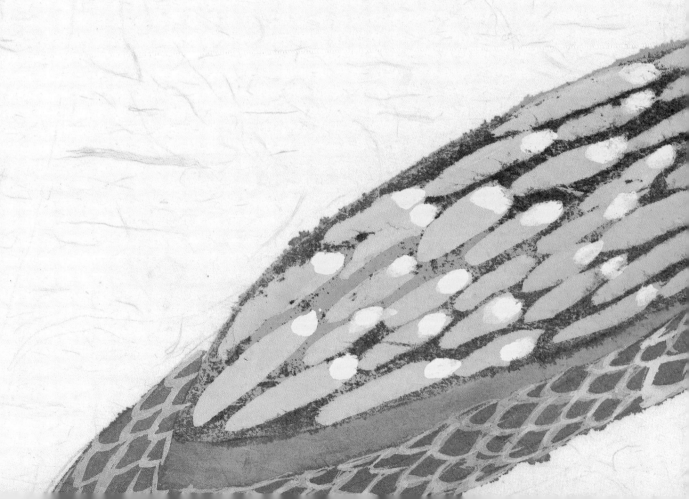

The ants kept on working.

"Silly ants," the grasshopper would say. "See the new moon. Feel the summer breeze. Let us go together and watch the Empress and her ladies as they prepare for midsummer's eve."

But the ants ignored the grasshopper and kept on working.

Soon the days grew shorter and the wind brought cooler air from the north. The ants, mindful of the winter to come, worked even harder to secure their home against the impending cold and snow. They foraged for food and brought it back to their nest, saving it for those cold winter months.

"Silly ants," said the grasshopper. "Don't you ever rest? Today is the harvest festival. The Emperor will feast on mooncakes and sweet greens from the fields. I will play my music for him until the moon disappears into the smooth lake water. Come and dance with me."

"You would do well to do as we do," said one of the ants. "Winter is coming soon and food will be hard to find. Snow will cover your house and you will freeze without shelter."

But the grasshopper ignored the ant's advice and continued to play and dance until the small hours of the morning.

Winter arrived a week later and brought whirls of snow and ice. The Emperor and his court left the Summer Palace for their winter home in the great Forbidden City. The ants closed their door against the ice and snow, safe and warm, resting at last after their long days of preparation.

And the grasshopper huddled
beneath the palace eaves and rubbed
his hands together in a mournful chirp,
wishing he had heeded the ant's advice.

AUTHOR'S NOTE

The original summer palace was called Yuanmingyuan, or "Garden of Perfect Brightness," and was built in 1747 during the Qing dynasty. Qianlong, the emperor at that time, commissioned Jesuit artisans to design this summer resort some six miles to the northwest of his permanent home, the Forbidden City, in Beijing. The buildings and grounds were modeled after European palaces in a Baroque style, complete with cascading fountains and extravagent pavilions. It served as a retreat for the emperor and his court during the hot summer months. The summer palace was later burned to the ground by French and English troops in 1860.

A later summer palace was built by the Dowager Empress Cixi in 1888. Called Yiheyuan, or "Garden for Cultivating Harmony," it was located about a mile west of the ruins of Yuanmingyuan, where it stands today.

I was fortunate to have spent four years, from 1990 to 1994, living with my family at the DaYuan Binguan located between the two palaces. We frequently visited both sites, exploring the ruins of Yuanmingyuan, picnicking near elaborately carved statues and pagodas, and, in winter, skating on the broad lake that lies in the middle of Yiheyuan.

The Ant and the Grasshopper is one of Aesop's Fables, a group of stories believed to have been written by a Greek slave named Aesop during the sixth century B.C.E. Many versions of this story have been retold throughout the ages. The summer palace seemed an ideal setting for a fable in which the changing of the seasons is so integral.

During my four years in China, I studied the craft of scroll making and worked with Chinese artists. To make these paintings, I applied ink and gouache to rice paper with traditional Chinese brushes. The paper was then flattened using a traditional method called Biao Huar, in which I mounted the drawings onto opaque rice paper using a homemade wheat-based glue.